Yoki the Yelling Yak

Written and Illustrated
by Lori Kaiser

Another great book in the Xavier Series!

Published by
Fleming Publishing
18204 Cooper Road
Conroe, TX 77302
281-635-2395

www.flemingpublishing.com

© Copyright, 2012 by Fleming Publishing. All Rights Reserved. No portion of this book may be reproduced, stored in a retrieval system, or transmitted, in any form or by any means, electronic, mechanical, photocopying, recording, or otherwise without prior written permission from publisher.
Printed in the United States of America
ISBN 978-0-9883770-1-1

Dedicated to my cousin, Casey Franklin. Always remember: Dare to be different and follow your dreams. Life gets tough, so make sure you let God lead the way. I love you so much and you are always in my prayers.

Here's a little story
that I really must tell.
It's about a yak named Yoki
and his obsessive need to yell.

He knew that when he talked,
he was a little loud.
He then decided he would try
to turn the volume down.

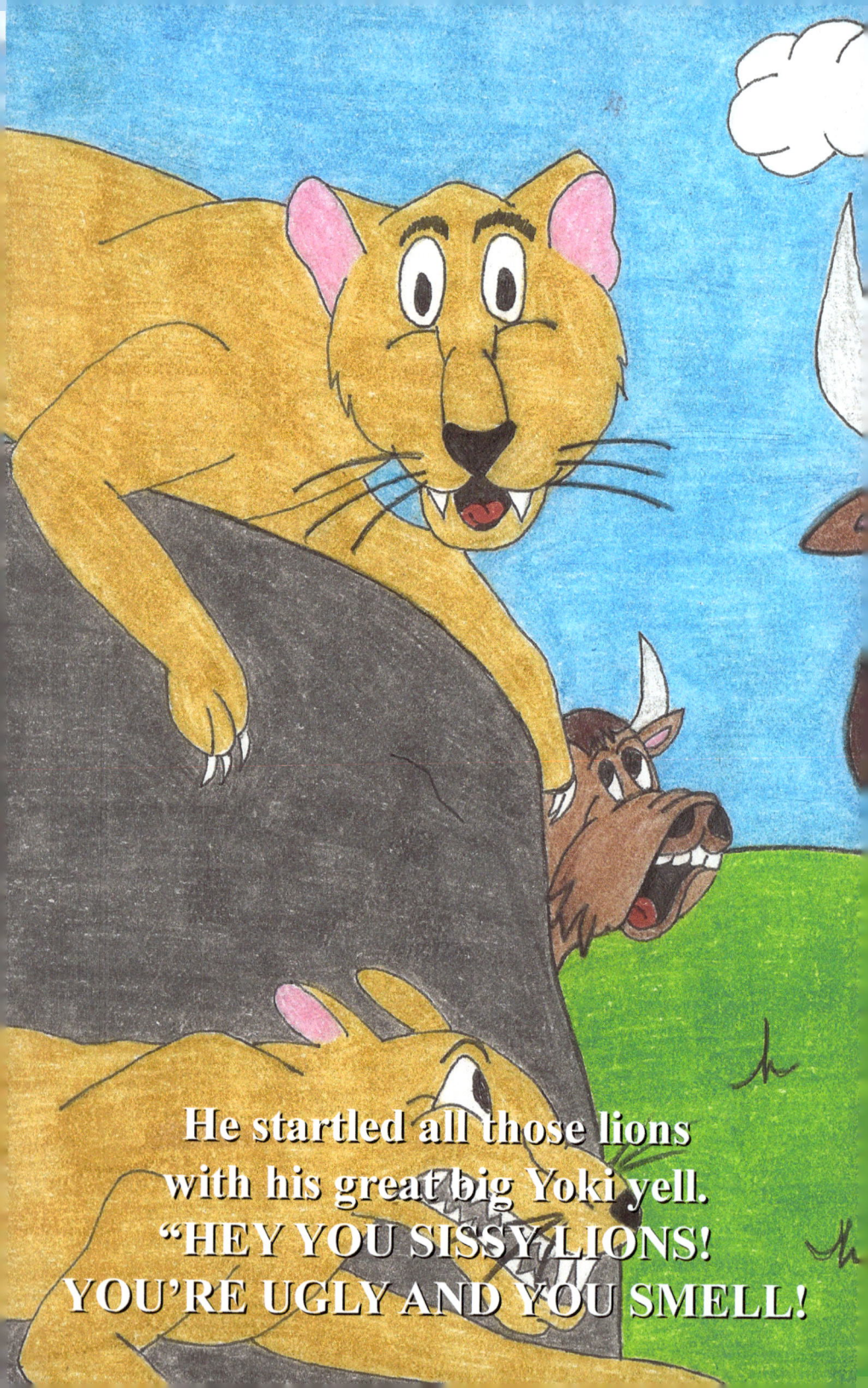

The lions took their big ole paws and covered up their ears.